FORGETTING HOW TO FLY

FORGETTING HOW TO FLY

MARK LOWEY

THISTLEDOWN PRESS

Canadian Cataloguing in Publication Data

Lowey, Mark, 1949-
    Forgetting How to Fly
Poems.

ISBN 0-920633-28-5 (bound).
ISBN 0-920633-29-3 (pbk).

I. Title.
PS8573.093F6 1987 C811'.54 C87-098025-4
PR9199.3.L69F6 1987

Book design by A. M. Forrie
Cover painting by Doug Thiell

Typeset by Pièce de Résistance, Edmonton
Set in 11 point Century Old Style

Printed and bound in Canada by
Hignell Printing Ltd., Winnipeg

Thistledown Press Ltd.
668 East Place
Saskatoon, Saskatchewan
S7J 2Z5

Acknowledgements

Some of these poems have appeared in: *Alberta Poetry Yearbook, Anthology of Magazine,Verse & Yearbook of American Poetry, Antigonish Review, Ariel, blue buffalo, Camrose Review, Canadian Author & Bookman, Cross-Canada Writers' Quarterly, Dandelion, event, Fiddlehead, Germination, Grain, Interface, NeWest Review, Poetry Canada Review, Quarry, Scrivener, Waves*, and *Whetstone*, and have been broadcast on CBC's "Alberta Anthology".

Thanks to Hector Williamson, Dave Margoshes, Christopher Wiseman and Robert Kroetsch for their encouragement and editorial assistance. Thanks also to Allan Forrie, who helped edit the final manuscript.

This book has been published with the assistance of the Alberta Foundation for the Literary Arts, the Canada Council and the Saskatchewan Arts Board.

for my family

for Pat

for Elona, who also
woos the sky

CONTENTS

TIN ROOF ANGELS

BIRDSONGS FOR THE DYING

TIN ROOF ANGELS

Dusk, cloud-printed
sky closes on land,
cover of a dark book.
Inside, the old
relate their story
for what it's worth,
memorize the words
binding them to earth.
Furrows unravel,
farm houses take root
by gravel roads
where mowers rust;
husks of car bodies
hunch in the field,
mottled dogs chase the sun
as the town discovers
its one hotel:
paint it green and brown.
Riders murmur, jackets sway,
sink sloshes water, sounds
fold around the day.
Too far from earth, airplane
will never know this ground
hugging the train to breast,
rocking, scolding it along,
hard mother.

Horizon surprises the eye:
water tanks, starched
elevators, wooden platform
with its clutch of people,
spaces waiting to be filled.

Patience at abandoned places:
withered grass pokes
fingers in the belly
of a forgotten boxcar,
weathered churches hold
faithfully to ghost town.
All the time, Number One West
clings to the rails like prayer
as if they really lead somewhere,
veering away as if
direction had a purpose.
Pickup trucks idle at crossroads
where thick wives corral husbands:
their peaked hats cleave the wind
and arms wave thin
as strips of leather;
these fertile couples
stubborn as thistle,
all their children
scattered like seed.

Beside a riverbank
of ankle-high grass,
dandelion undermined
by impatient current,
that brushcut boy
dips an Orange Crush bottle
into the swirls.

That's how he's caught:
leaning toward the camera,
one foot lost to water
one foot hidden
in the lush bank.
His eyes, expectant,
take in the photographer.
His raised hand
holds the half-filled bottle;
a smile eddies along his lips.

Swamped by his father's
hand-me-down swim trunks,
the thin boy bends
to the sweet, stubborn ignorance
of his thirteen years,
barely moving toward
abandoned riversides,
empty riverbeds.

Perhaps it's only
an angle of light,
the position
of the photographer:
but right there
there
the light
behind his eyes
already reflects
the sad glitter
of broken glass.

Smooth bare feet
smack on their dare,
slap through a puddle
of second thoughts;
hands grip ladder rungs,
hold fast
their hollow taunt.

Climb and climb
until you finally stand
on the long, white slab;
stutter of false starts,
heart drowning and
no spit for your voice.
The ceiling is webbed
like an old man's face,
eyes grown weary
measuring the gap.
Miles below, boys
swim tight circles,
smelling blood.
You force your legs
along the board, out
to the edge of nothing:
rebound your body, discover
Newton's sudden science,
the scream to water.

What remains is silence,
memory of lungs
timed to limbs
curving the element
like a smile, a scythe;
nightmare of bottom
kicking hooves
through your chest,
a heaving for surface,
a holding of breath.

Sixty feet of sandstone
hidden from the city,
our secret place
where water and prairie
conspired in danger,
plunged like buffalo
driven over the edge.
I tiptoed them
along the crest,
taunted their height,
climbed with the others
up from a creek
to a bend where it carved
memories of rivers.

They would never catch us:
booting toeholds in the sky,
fleeing the classroom posse,
life sentences to memorize;
desperadoes, our ledges crumbling
in relentless sun,
rush of years, the roar
beneath our feet.

In the field
with gopher flankers,
grasshopper ends,
we played football.
I was a one-rule manager:
everybody plays,
even beagle Toby
barking out signals;
little kids afraid of the game
served as wandering goalposts.
Neighbourhood mothers
thought me possessed
or godsent: lining up
their summertime runaways
into ragamuffin defence,
ragtag offence,
racing them to exhaustion.

My peers mocked their way
to dances, backseat touch.
Their eyes shouldered me
against gymnasium walls,
marked me separate.
But in the field
I was never alone.

I stand here years later,
catch shades running patterns
through tall grass;
the sun wobbles
to the shout
of touchdowns, fumbles,
no one is keeping score.

Intimidated by dandelion
Russian thistle and dust,
the wilderness has been tamed:
four perplexed buffalo,
three gummy timber wolves
with the moon tucked
between their legs,
two lumpy llama,
one pestered badger,
half-a-dozen dozy pigs,
eight tattered chickens,
one chicken-feathered white man
peddling balsa wood tomahawks,
one sway-backed nag
staked to a circle
for two bits a ride,
one broken-down ferris wheel
bullied by the wind;
woeful menagerie
fronted by a sign:

Moose Jaw Wild Animal Park
No Dogs Allowed

You are bound hand and foot
hanging by your teeth
from the branch of a tree
leaning out over Saskatchewan

Beginning at the myth:
Daedalus and Icarus, confined
to the grey light of Knossos,
sought the sun, designed

wings worthy of an angel.
Down the labyrinth of halls
Daedalus bent upon labour,
Icarus dreamed above walls.

Daedalus feathered flight
with reason, mindful of the heat.
Icarus soared on faith, heedless
of seas beneath his feet.

Father rose on pinions
to the height that freedom brings.
We are sons of son, captives
to half-completed wings.

Your best shot
buckled the legs
of the white-tailed deer,
sent its flight
crashing to earth.
Your son ran to it,
raised its head, felt the blood
ebb beneath the fur.
He heard spirits
whisper through the trees,
knew they lingered
in dull brown eyes,
in legs kicking
for that distant hill.
You knelt beside him,
stilled his tears
with your fingers
red at the deer's throat.

Next season
you sold your rifle.
When your son wanted
a gun for Christmas
you carved a pistol
that would never fire,
its spruce barrel aimed
at his open heart.

Tar-paper strips flutter
free of the roof,
drape like giant bat wings
over the willow tree.
I could have died
seventeen times today:
stopped shingling and
flung my absurdly winged body
toward the sun.
I would have livened up
a half-dead afternoon
for all the neighbours
who stood pointing,
awaiting my fatal footslip.
I can hear them now
as the ambulance rushes me
to Emergency, wings akimbo:

He seemed like such a nice boy.
He was doing such a good job
fixing up the house.

Oh, yeah? Look at all this
old tar-paper on my sidewalk,
complains next-door-Ike,
who leaves scrawled grievances
taped to my front door.
What was he doing up there
in the first place?
wonders down-the-street-Bev,

who studies logic at university
and likes to keep death
in its proper perspective.

I hang before them
between sea and sky,
this place I've always been.
Newborn breeze
lifts another bat wing,
blows it to the water.
Waves lick my feet.
I throw my hammer at the sun,
I raise my wings
believing I will fly.

Stretched to utmost tiptoes
he still can't reach it,
shuffles to the corner
on his cross-legged jig.
Big brother zips up his fly,
tells the little guy
he'll have to wait:
it's a man's world
of raised urinals,
all cubicles occupied.
    But I got to pee . . .
Big brother scolds the whimper,
smacks the clutched hands
from the small one's crotch.

Over my shoulder
I look for a pail, a board,
anything to let him stand tall.
But the empty floor
denies a rescue.
Suddenly the door swings wide:
a man's eyes dart
to the dribbler's dance;
he lifts his son
off the floor,
hoists him over the urinal
and says: Let 'er rip.
I smile, but feel an ache
in my own strong arms
that know nothing
of such weight.

My father, we turn
atop a high tin roof,
speak of ground so distant
it must be imagined;
our talk becomes
the family story,
passed to each generation.

Frantically we race:
nail tin sheets to
separate sides of the roof,
stumble over the clatter
of time, the rhythm
of the second hammer
asking how far
each of us has come.

Your dark hair in the wind
unravels like entrails;
I read your fortune.
Finally we lose patience,
stare at each other
as the immense structure
where we stand
begins to buckle.

We flap our arms together,
forgetting how to fly.
I run to your side,
nail your palms to the sky.

Six o'clock news ladles
disaster with dinner:
tourists caught at the top
of this foreign hotel
in rooms where they'll spend
the rest of their lives;
real version of Hollywood's
Towering Inferno.
My fork scrapes
against a scream
lingering like smoke,
men die helpless
calling for mother.
People hungry for air
leap from windows,
my mouth swallows
shards of glass;
the camera follows
a dark-haired angel,
his wings unfolding
a fiery pinwheel
plunging to the street.

When I was a boy
I was never afraid
of high places.
I lived in my tree house
on the edge of cliffs.
My mother always
told me she prayed
that if I fell
I would die of fear
before I hit bottom.

Echo Lake is that distant world
of ice, this name frozen
on my lips.
Snow fills the afternoon,
the margins of silence;
slowly the sun climbs Haeckel Hill,
cold grips the spruce.
The dogs patrol the forest,
bark at anyone
who isn't family.
My father and uncle saw
firewood, split kindling,
remember the railroad
and the great iron wheels
raised with their hands.
They brush the snow away,
white clings to their hair.
My mother's pans of water
tick on the Franklin stove,
windows unravel
constellations of frost.
She darns grey woollen socks,
mixes suet for jays
that eat from her fingers;
she sleeps five hours a night
and never stops moving,
all her dreams
impatient for spring.

That rainy Monday afternoon
you drove out from the city
to pick me up:
I was tired again
of the job, the people, the day.
Hunched beneath the overhang
of a church roof,
I watched your blue Ford
round the corner
and skid to where I stood,
waiting for deliverance.

C'mon, let's go shoot some pool.
Pooool? you said,
like you had no time for pool.

But I saw you smile
beneath your bushy moustache
as you flipped the quarter
to see who would break.

Only the tigers
are not afraid
of the tractor.
They sense my approach
before hearing it,
already risen
from watchful sleep
to face me.

The ravens become
crazed shadows
clawing corners
from the air,
the bears cower
like bedside teddies,
even the timber wolf
paces his cell,
counting the end.

Only the tigers
follow along the fence
where I mow the grass,
tractor lights
blinking a warning
under myriad reckonings
of tiger eyes.

When I'm through
only the fence
stays their fantasy.
But down the road,
cutting a boulevard
on a busy street,
I look up, see them
crouched to spring,
eyes wide with
holes in the fence.

You flickered in a sky
dark as the span between stars,
endless as the time
before morning
when an empty bed
grows vast with longing:
our clothes tangled
as the knots we tied
in each other's lives,
our eager hands
closing the distance.

How could we escape
that room where you knelt
to say childhood prayers?
Your mother blocked the way
with her bottle and Bible,
commandments of glass;
your father with his wheelchair,
bad back and spirit broken
on seams of coal.
Now I lay them
down to sleep
in north Saskatchewan.

You were sixteen,
hungry for places
you wouldn't have to share;
I was a year older, dreamed

I could take you there.
But when you were asleep
I saw your mother and father
creep into the room,
slip into our clothes
and stand over the bed,
wearing our faces like masks.
I left the wind
to marry your sighs,
followed the sound
of a rig gearing down
to take on a ride.

window on the sea
stars adrift
    impossible
harbour of the sky

a moth clings to
reflections in the pane
Crusoe fluttering
upon shoals of light

slivers of light
strung like a wreck
across the page

                    Vancouver

BIRDSONGS FOR THE DYING

Her family hurries past,
throngs to miracles
proclaimed along the midway:
Ride the Tidal Wave,
Toss the Ring,
Escape the Haunted Mansion.
She lingers in the Agri-Building
at the poultry display,
fingers clutching chicken wire,
eyes on china shells.

Two hours, the attendant says,
before that bunch will hatch.
Impatient teen, he plucks
an egg from the table's edge,
chucks it in the garbage.
Been there since Tuesday, he says.
Some don't make it.
She's only ten, she tells him,
she has time to wait.

She does not move
until the chick
opens a hole
on this blind world,
widens the window
where sky breaks through,
shy tip of wing
catching on her cry.

I

You going to Beatlemania?
(that road show from Chicago:
four American lads
who resemble The Beatles,
play music that almost
sounds like the real thing
while a larger-than-life screen
flickers with the ghosts
of the Sixties:
Ed Sullivan, Walt Disney,
the Kennedy brothers,
Martin Luther King)

I don't know.
(I got lost for a while,
having my hair cut
by this talkative brunette
who's from Winnipeg,
Windsor Park to be exact.
In 1965 I lived in the North End,
the other side of the tracks,
on welfare and in love
with Lady Madonna. Windsor Park
was a developer's dream)

II

It's the day's small miracle
she's so friendly;
delicate Japanese birds
on her silk blouse
rustle by my ears
like breeze through Manitoba maple
a decade and a half from here.
She's not like Otto
who's on vacation
to the old country,
whose rough German hands
worry my scalp
with fingers unrelenting
as suburban streets.

III

So you going?

*I don't know.
How much will it cost?*

*Thirteen dollars.
I've already got my ticket.
I can hardly wait.*

*I don't know. I haven't been
for a long time.
I guess the real four will never
get back together now.*

*No. Besides,
aren't two of them dead?
The others must be nearly forty.*

IV

She snips a thread
in my thoughts;
for the first time I look
past the birds on her blouse
and into her face,
see she's made up
to appear much older
but she's barely twenty.

I think of that
larger-than-life screen:
the collapse of Camelot,
secret service men clinging
to the trunk of a car,
Hey, Jude, take a sad song
and will they do Paperback Writer
for all the notes which have sat
on my desk for fifteen years?

No, I don't think I'll go.
Hey, don't take any more
off the top.

Calgary, summer, 1980

Breathless in the tree
she has climbed for joy
to be a little nearer the sun:
the bride prays,
patient as ritual.
She feels the seed
branching inside,
meets the smiles of guests
who look up, ask
how many children?
As many as there are
leaves in this tree.

Soldiers arrive like winter.
Pieces of bread fall
from severed hands,
husbands disappear forever
in the backs of trucks;
wives with machetéd feet
crawl from uniformed men
pinning them again and again.
She hides in the thickest boughs
of the tree,
dreaming of her groom:
his conspiracies whisper,
gather in her heart.
She picks a single leaf
and holds it to her breast;
his body greens the hills,
blood nurtures the seed.

The wind argues, twists
his white shirt like a riddle,
a flag for no country.
On a reporter's hunch
Bill reaches the roadblock,
holds his press card
high against merciless sun.
A soldier pushes through the ranks,
slams a rifle barrel
to Bill's temple:
the camera keeps running,
the shot splatters his brain
into living rooms
across the world.

Like a scorpion, this country
walks backward, hunting itself.
Rubble cradles children,
strangers to cartoon death;
here it is real
as the sting in the belly,
a missing older brother.
Reason is impenetrable
like the jungle
probing Bill's body,
his mouth open
on the next question.

The old man hunches
on the park bench,
a cliché for the young.
His friends hover
near as memory, share
the white-winged blur
of all his years.
On the ground
a heap of day-old bagels
he barters for a story;
he cranes his neck to hear,
the pigeons woo him
with the sky.

I am above and
over the old man's back,
cradling a telephoto:
the only closeness
I can manage.
I spy a second old man
alight on the bench,
together they coo
conspiracies of age.
The old always have
too much to say,
not enough time to tell.

My camera eavesdrops.
I take their picture,
reluctant to move on
to other sights.
I will return too soon
to my own country,
where young men are found
frozen on park benches
or seen for the last time:
a remote speck
standing in the prairie,
intent upon wings.

(St. Joseph's Oratory, Montreal)

Inside the basilica
the contest proclaims:
Win a Free Trip to Rome!
Witness the Beatification!
For forty cents, visitors
light a candle, pray
for family harmony, happy death.
For a bigger request
(the conversion of someone
who has gone astray)
candles are larger
to match the price.
Awed tourists pay
to weigh themselves,
see a religious wax museum.
Souvenir shops sell
thirty-five dollar posters:
Brother Andre beside his towels,
bowl and toe rubbers;
signs invite the faithful
to view his funeral
live on the screen
for only ten cents, or buy
three-dimensional colour photos
of Christ on the cross.
When the photo is tilted
Christ's blue eyes
blink open and shut.

You killed for money:
here are two coins
for the lids of your eyes,
staring at the camera
from court to the cell
where there's no room to pose
and all you count is time.
Prison is medicine
works best in the dark:
under cover of a Kingston night
someone will cut
the truth from your skin,
unconvinced though you twist
like a thief at confession.

I can't linger
between acts, hoping
to catch your eyes
like half-heard lines,
or chance meeting you
with a greeting
stilted as that mouthed
by the greenest ingenue.

I know my repertoire:
I can alter my voice,
add the required distance,
subtract it like
excess dialogue;
adept at body semaphore,
I can move my arms
to corresponding emotions.

But I'm not so accomplished
I can pretend
I don't want you,
bare-thighed
behind the stage
with all the masks
ripped away.

We find shelter
in forest cathedral,
this driving snow
sudden as lust:
underwear adrift
around our ankles,
two cheeks to the wind
I hop like a magpie
on stiff legs,
push you against the trunk
of a trembling aspen.
The wind speaks winter,
offers love no reason,
but your hot tongue
tells of another season.

If only I had
a second pair of hands,
fingers that weren't
turning blue on your ass:
they could hold a camera,
take a shot
of our stormy coupling.
We would make up postcards
titled *Spring Has Sprung*,
send them to everyone
this Sunday blizzard
has numbed to prayer.

Stars show the way
clear as intention;
they did that night
we drove through reflection,
found a dark road
beyond the city,
past interference
from our street-lit lives.
We sheltered on the hood,
backs against the windshield:
sky traffic spilled
down the Milky Way
until a celestial traveller
chilled by care
struck a match
and a meteor flared.

I leaned into space,
you into me,
arms circling like rings.
I warmed my hands
on your breasts,
your body turned
with more purpose
than a world.

You come apart
when you see it:
  What the hell is
  that huge bump
  on your shirt?!

My famous scar stitch:
using a needle with an eye
you could push
a basketball through,
basic black thread
over and over in loops.
Not pretty, but
it holds things and
when you touch it,
it reminds you,
like a scar.

Laughing, you took over
for too long a time;
infinitely patient,
you made the repairs.
I watched how you did it.
It took years
but I learned to sew
and we unravelled
a little each day.

ON LIVING WITH CHILDREN
FOR A PROLONGED TIME

Now I know
why God ordered Abe
to bump off Isaac.
Not that God
was pulling rank
or had created the ultimate
test of faith:
just that Isaac was
such an unruly little bastard,
and God, of course,
had to keep His nose clean.

Now I know
why the normally stoic Greeks
hurled their newborn
like dialogues and theorems
from high cliff foreheads.

Now I know
the bloody brotherhood
of stooped Herod
who parted the reeds,
as I dipped my hands
in the bulrush slaughter.

They come in the front door,
unlace running shoes
almost as big as mine,
appraise me from pillbox eyes,
force a reticent hello
through lips
pressed down tight.
The hall silence bristles
with their thoughts of me,
mine of them.

I want to tell them
I'm not dangerous,
I'm not the enemy.
But they sidestep me,
armoured as they pass,
follow him downstairs.

Does he defend me
Nah, he ain't so bad.
or is he one of them?
Yeah, he's out of it, man.
Do sides need taking
between him and me?
I don't know anymore,
don't know if I ever did.

They thunder
through my thoughts
back upstairs:
Catch ya later, hey.
And they're gone,
leaving me weighted
with years and questions.

My son
my son
those shoes at the door
so big
so big to fill.

TIME CORRODES THE HEART

(On burying radioactive waste)

Trees writhe
on gnarled roots,
ebony cats criss-
cross this field,
silent as an empty crib.
They go through earth
on paws hooked
with claws of madness.
Their mouths gape, glowing
teeth carve holes
in embryos.
Cries poison the wind,
a hurricane
of mutant children
storms the womb.

Don't call it sadness,
this orphan shiver
born at your lips.
Don't call it anything.

I am not sad
when I surprise you
with my mouth.
I am not sad
we are silent
like voices lost
beneath the sea.
I trace the way your breath
meets my breath, together
we break the surface.
I am not sad
even when I find
this shiver on your lips;
not until I ask,
not until you name it,
not until we realize
there are words.

This is the poem
I meant to write
for your fortieth birthday.
But I could not find
appropriate words,
a line that would
untangle our years,
hieroglyph of hands
reaching their sad conclusion:
we will never become
all we thought we could be.
I grope my way,
feel for verses
blind as a lie.

The truth is
I lean into shadows
cast by your light,
lower my face on your breast
and your body speaks
in an ancient tongue.
The truth is
I wake, when the sun
escapes through the shutter
and wonder that I am
still in our bed,
inventing the language
to leave you.

Sylvia
when your head
burned through by blue light
was in the oven
did you think
of the poem you would write
the next morning,
did you think
like all women
you look more lovely
having left these men
who left you first:
father husband son
Holy Ghost

Hooded chickadees cling
to winter, balance
on filaments of sky,
lines that bind us
to our place;
them to the air,
us to earth, resigned
to solid ground.
They sing
to the dying afternoon
falling like a stone
on the horizon,
our light contained
by a certain darkness.
You shift to your knees,
untie me bare and
circle me with wings,
your mouth taking hold,
pulling me
away from the world.
A chickadee persists
at the sunflower bell
until down its throat
seeds disappear
like bronze fish,
the sky catches fire
in your hair.

More distance in death than
light-years unravelling
between Earth and star,
more by far than time
stitching child to the man.

Mortality makes us
partners, hands out
black shoes to dance
beyond tomorrow's riddle
or reel of circumstance.

Death reaches bony-fingered
from corners of the womb
to grasp our fleshy palms,
whirl our days
around the room

where lines of the living
stand, wide-eyed
at this demon of a dancer
leading another
without pause to decide

whom to swing out the door.
Every death is a dance,
terrible jig of distance
lifting each a little farther
from the floor.

I build a fence without gates,
a walled city where
there is always
one loose stone, entrances
hinged on air.
Beyond my walls
a procession of torches
burns across the Earth,
pickets split the sun
into islands of orange.
I build a house
with a blue roof
the sky peeks through,
windows where the trees
look in, eyes that open
on the world.
When it rains
the clouds unfurl
flags for the storm,
let down
ladders of mist.
Leaves hold their palms
in prayer,
in photosynthesis;
good secrets
take forever to know.

I stand at the threshold
peering in
and inside out,
clench my teeth
in arctic air
or feel the equatorial breeze,
perfumed like a woman,
breathe against my skin.
My hands blister
as I build,
I cannot satisfy
my longing for precision.
I tell myself
even the sun is not perfect;
my hammer frames the eclipse,
darkness laughs in my mouth.

Now you have heard them
you will never escape:
the conspiracy of horses
breaks from the gate,
gallops through the night.
Listen to them pace.
When you turn your back
they'll neigh at your heels,
deny complicity,
join a carousel,
cloud mirrors as they race.

Time will settle on your shoulders
gentle as a sparrow
you'll try but never catch.
Highways will unravel
beneath your own horsepower,
but there won't be room
to retrace your tracks
in case you missed a place
worth stopping for,
a face you should know.

You'll drive on for centuries.
Greeks at the walls will conspire
in the horse's belly,
every city will fall,
soldiers will follow the sun west
searching for places to die.
There are no good places left:
our intimate ruins
make us all lie down
where we least expect
to find ourselves.

I could never imagine
this hospital room, you
harnessed to tubes, stainless steel.
I can't feel the beast you straddle.
Even in sleep
you clench the sheets,
hang on for your life.
The conspiracy of horses
never stops to catch its breath.
Close your eyes so you do not see them:
though their hooves thunder
against your chest,
your wax-feathered wings
will fly you to Elysium.